First World War
and Army of Occupation
War Diary
France, Belgium and Germany

32 DIVISION
14 Infantry Brigade
King's (Liverpool Regiment)
52nd Graduated Battalion
15 March 1919 - 31 October 1919

WO95/2394/3

The Naval & Military Press Ltd
www.nmarchive.com
Published in association with The National Archives

Published by

The Naval & Military Press Ltd

Unit 10 Ridgewood Industrial Park,

Uckfield, East Sussex,

TN22 5QE England

Tel: +44 (0) 1825 749494

www.naval-military-press.com

www.nmarchive.com

This diary has been reprinted in facsimile from the original. Any imperfections are inevitably reproduced and the quality may fall short of modern type and cartographic standards.

© Crown Copyright
Images reproduced by permission of The National Archives, London, England, 2015.

Contents

Document type	Place/Title	Date From	Date To
Heading	WO95/2394 Mar-Oct '19 52 Kings Liverpool		
Heading	32 Div 14 Bde 52 K. L'Pool. R. 2188		
Heading	War Diary Commanding 15th March 1919) 52 Bn. The Kings (Liverpool) Regt. Army Of The Rhine.		
War Diary	Woodbridge Suffolk.	15/03/1919	15/03/1919
War Diary	Dover	16/03/1919	16/03/1919
War Diary	Qunkirk	17/03/1919	17/03/1919
War Diary	Obercassel by Bonn	19/03/1919	20/03/1919
War Diary	Romlinghoven	25/03/1919	25/03/1919
Heading	O. i/c No. 3 Starris Free Library Reserve Lancs England		
Heading			
War Diary	Obercassel Germany	01/05/1919	31/05/1919
War Diary	Obercassel Germany	01/05/1919	28/06/1919
War Diary	Obercassel Germany	19/06/1919	25/07/1919
War Diary	Obercassel Germany	04/07/1919	31/08/1919
War Diary	Obercassel Germany	01/08/1919	31/08/1919
War Diary	Obercassel	08/09/1919	30/09/1919
War Diary	Obercassel	01/09/1919	30/09/1919
Heading	War Diary (Commanding 15/3/19) 52 Bn The Kings (Liverpool) Regt. Vol I Jan 1920		
War Diary	Woodbridge Suffolk	15/03/1919	15/03/1919
War Diary	Dover	15/03/1919	15/03/1919
War Diary	Dunkirk	16/03/1919	17/03/1919
War Diary	Obercassel by Bonn	19/03/1919	25/03/1919
War Diary	Dunkirk	16/03/1919	16/03/1919
War Diary	Siegburg-Mulldorf	19/03/1919	19/03/1919
War Diary	Geistingen	22/03/1919	22/03/1919
War Diary	Dambroich	27/03/1919	27/03/1919
War Diary	Geistingen	30/03/1919	30/03/1919
War Diary	Obercassel Germany	04/04/1919	27/05/1919
War Diary	Obercassel Germany	01/05/1919	18/06/1919
War Diary	Birlinghoven	19/06/1919	28/06/1919
War Diary	Obercassel	19/06/1919	30/06/1919
War Diary	Obercassel Germany	02/07/1919	25/07/1919
War Diary	Obercassel Germany	02/07/1919	31/08/1919
War Diary	Obercassel Germany	01/08/1919	31/08/1919
War Diary	Obercassel	08/09/1919	30/09/1919
War Diary	Obercassel	08/09/1919	31/10/1919
Operation(al) Order(s)	52nd. Bn. "The King's" Order No. 4.	15/10/1919	15/10/1919
Operation(al) Order(s)	52nd King's Addendum No. 1 To Order No. 4	16/10/1919	16/10/1919
Operation(al) Order(s)	52nd. Bn. "The Kings" Liverpool Regt. Order No. 1	26/10/1919	26/10/1919
Operation(al) Order(s)	52nd Bn King's Liverpool Regt. Order No. 2	26/10/1919	26/10/1919
Operation(al) Order(s)	52nd Bn King's Liverpool Regiment. Order No. 3	26/10/1919	26/10/1919

WO 95/2394
Mar - Oct '19
52 Kings Liverpool
③

BEF
32 DIV
14 Bde

52 K. L'Pool R.

2188

31 DIV Rawalpindi

WAR DIARY
or
~~INTELLIGENCE SUMMARY~~

Army Form C. 2118.

Duplicate

War Diary (commencing 15th March 1919)

52 Bn. The King's (Liverpool) Regt.

Army of the Rhine.

Army Form C. 2118.

WAR DIARY
or
INTELLIGENCE SUMMARY.
(Erase heading not required.)

Place	Date	Hour	Summary of Events and Information	Remarks and references to Appendices
WOODBRIDGE SUFFOLK.	15/3/19	10.55	Unit entrains for Dover, 41 Officers 762. O. Ranks.	
DOVER.	16/3/19	19.00	Detains for Dunkirk.	
		09.00	Embarked for Dunkirk.	
DUNKIRK.		12.00	Disembarked & proceeded to No 3 Camp.	
	17/3/19	09.00	Entrained for Germany. (Strength 41 Officers 762. O.Rs.)	
OBERCASSEL by BONN.	19/3/19	07.00	Detrained.	
	20/3/19		Takes over Billets, Transport, Stores of 1st DORSET Regt.	
ROTTING HOVEN.	25/3/19		"A" Coy 5th K'NGS resumes command of Outpost Post on Outpost Linesvice "C" Coy 1st DORSET REGT.	

(Sgd) A. Atkern W6C
Comg. 32nd The King's Regt.

Army Form C. 2118.

WAR DIARY
or
INTELLIGENCE SUMMARY.
(Erase heading not required.)

Instructions regarding War Diaries and Intelligence Summaries are contained in F. S. Regs., Part II. and the Staff Manual respectively. Title pages will be prepared in manuscript.

No. 7914
10 JUN 1919
SESSIONS HOUSE

Place	Date	Hour	Summary of Events and Information	Remarks and references to Appendices
OBERCASSEL GERMANY	1/5/19	08.00	Practice defence scheme; code word POSITIONS received at 08.00. Last company in position, all stores, kitpost etc. ready by 09.30 hours. All communications worked well & necessary reports were despatched with promptitude.	
	2/5/19	14.30	Conference with G.O.C. Division at King's Brigade H.Q. ref. defence scheme.	
	7/5/19		MAJOR C.E.R.G. ALBAN D.S.O. assumes command of the Battalion this day, vice Lt. Col. A.H. SPOONER C.M.G., D.S.O. proceeded to take over command of 15th LANCS. FUSILIERS.	
	8/5/19		Outpost line advanced to include DOLLENDORFER HARDT.	
	13/5/19		Battalion shows present at Gen. C's inspection of units of LANCS. DIVISION at HANGELAR AERODROME.	
	14/5/19		"B" Company mounts Divisional Guard at BONN.	
	16/5/19		Marshal FOCH visits British force; arrived by river from COBLENZ. Battalion paraded in full strength on river bank at OBERCASSEL.	
	18/5/19		Officers' mounted paper chase; 24 starters.	
	23/5/19		Brigadier inspects "A" Company in tactical scheme.	
	27/5/19		Rest route march of 10 miles, full marching order.	
	31/5/19		Battalion Strength Officers 49 + 2 attached O.Rs. 1103 + 3 "	
	1/5/19 TO 31/5/19		Individual + Platoon training carried out.	

W.E.J. Kitson
Lt. Col.
Cmdg. 52nd B. L. "The King's"

Army Form C. 2118.

WAR DIARY
or
INTELLIGENCE SUMMARY.

(Erase heading not required.)

Instructions regarding War Diaries and Intelligence Summaries are contained in F. S. Regs., Part II. and the Staff Manual respectively. Title pages will be prepared in manuscript.

Place	Date	Hour	Summary of Events and Information	Remarks and references to Appendices
OBERCASSEL GERMANY.	3/6/19	-	Special Battalion Parade in honour of The King's Birthday.	
	2/6/19 3/6/19		Inter-company musketry competition on 200ˣ range	
			Brigade Rifle Meeting on 200ˣ range. 52ⁿᵈ Kings won 2 battalion competitions	
	14/6/19 5/6/19		Musketry & photo meeting 32ⁿᵈ Kings v 51 Manchesters at BIRLINGHOYEN. 52ⁿᵈ Kings won by 1 point.	
	15/6/19		Confirmation of J day received. Action taken in accordance with orders known by	
			All surplus stores, kits etc taken to rear dump at BONN (J-2 day)	
	19/6/19		J-1 day. Battalion moves to BIRLINGHOVEN. - Less D Coy, who remain on outpost duty at RÖMMINGHOVEN. Leave OBERCASSEL 0.10 hours, fighting order, arrive BIRLINGHOVEN 12.00 hours. Troops in close billets for the night.	
	28/6/19	18.00	Peace Treaty signed. News received 18.00 hours.	
	19/6/19 28/6/19		Company & specialist training carried out at BIRLINGHOVEN.	
	30/6/19		"A" Coy. Battalion returns to original billets in OBERCASSEL.	

STRENGTH OF BATTALION ON 30/6/19 OFFICERS 48 + 2 attached
O.R. 1123 + 2 attached
Officer 31 + 2 attached
Ranks. 889 + 1 attached

Fighting Strength of Battalion 30/6/19.

CRMKing Lt.Col.
C.mdg. 52 Kings

Army Form C. 2118.

WAR DIARY
or
INTELLIGENCE SUMMARY.

(Erase heading not required.)

Instructions regarding War Diaries and Intelligence Summaries are contained in F. S. Regs., Part II. and the Staff Manual respectively. Title pages will be prepared in manuscript.

July, 1919.

Place	Date	Hour	Summary of Events and Information	Remarks and references to Appendices
OBERCASSEL GERMANY	4/7/19		Brigade Rifle Meeting – six inter-Battalion events. 52nd King's won four events & obtained 1 second & 1 third place.	
	5/7/19		"B" Company Sports.	
	6/7/19		"A" Company Sports.	
	7/7/19		The Commanding Officer proceeds to Paris as O.R.C. to B.G. Commanding Rhine Army troops taking part in the Victory March. Major F.W. Jelham assumes command of the Bn. Four N.C.O.'s proceeded to Paris to represent this Bn. in the Victory March.	
	9/7/19		Brigade Boxing competition won by 52nd King's.	
	15/7/19	14.00	Swimming Gala. Water Polo Match for points towards Bde. Championship Shield. 52nd King's obtained first place.	
	17/7/19		"A" & "B" Coys proceeded on Rhine Trip.	
	18/7/19		Lt.Col. Alban D.S.O. returns from Paris.	
	21/7/19		Very successful Battalion Sports held on RÖMLINGHOVEN ground. Inter Company Sports Cup was won by "D" Coy.	
	23/7/19		Brigade Sports Meeting. The Battn. obtained first place in Mile Relay Cross Country Race. Tug-of-War & Transport. The 52nd King's thus won the Brigade Commander's Shield, by a margin of 6 points.	
	25/7/19		Major F.W. Jelham assumes command of the Bn. vice Lt.Col. E.W.P. Alban proceeded on leave to U.K.	
	1-31/7/19		Battalion Coy. Training carried out – G.W.C. commenced.	
	31/7/19		Battalion strength 48 officers – 1073 O.R. 2 Officers attached.	

J.S. Rathe
Major
Comdg. 52nd King's

Duplicate

Army Form C. 2118.

WAR DIARY
or
INTELLIGENCE SUMMARY.
(Erase heading not required.)

Instructions regarding War Diaries and Intelligence Summaries are contained in F. S. Regs., Part II. and the Staff Manual respectively. Title pages will be prepared in manuscript.

Place	Date	Hour	Summary of Events and Information	Remarks and references to Appendices
OBERCASSEL.	5.8.19.		Brigade Hockey Match : 13th Kings beat 52nd Kings. 1-0.	
GERMANY.	10.8.19.		Divisional Challenge Cup : Tug of War : Heavy weight 52nd Kings beat 13th Kings. Light weight 52nd Kings beat 13th Kings.	
	14.8.19.		Battalion proceeded on Rhine trip to COBLENZ.	
	16.8.19.		"A" Company took over Outpost line & billets at VINXEL.	
	18.8.19.		Lt. Col. L.E.A.G. Alban. DSO resumed command of Battalion on return from leave.	
	22.8.19.		1 Officer & 5 other ranks proceeded on tour of ARRAS Battlefields.	
			Divisional Cross Country Run : 52nd Kings gained 2nd place.	
	27.8.19.		Divisional Horse Show : 52nd Kings gained 1 first (Officers Ride & Drive) & 2 thirds.	
	31.8.19.		Presentation of medals by G.O.C. Brigade to winners in Brigade Sports.	
	1-31.8.19.		Battalion & Company training carried on.	
			"A" & "B" Companies completed G.M.C.	
			"B" Company commenced G.M.C.	
	31.8.19.		Battalion Strength : 47 Officers. 1006 Other Ranks.	
			2 Officers attached.	

L/Col Alban h/u
Cmdg 52nd The Kings Regt.

Army Form C. 2118.

WAR DIARY
or
INTELLIGENCE SUMMARY.
(Erase heading not required.)

Instructions regarding War Diaries and Intelligence Summaries are contained in F. S. Regs., Part II. and the Staff Manual respectively. Title pages will be prepared in manuscript.

Place	Date	Hour	Summary of Events and Information	Remarks and references to Appendices
OBERCASSEL	8/9/19 to 13/9/19		RHINE ARMY RIFLE MEETING. 52nd KINGS succeeded in securing 4 Cups (3 firsts 1 second) 9 4·5 Medals.	
	16/9/19		TUG OF WAR. 52nd KINGS beat 5th Bordons then winning Divisional Final.	
	17/9/19		TUG OF WAR. 63rd R.G.A. beat 52nd KINGS in Army Semi-Final.	
	22/9/19		CORPS AQUATIC SPORTS: 52nd KINGS won 2 Firsts, 2 Seconds & 1 Third.	
	23/9/19		FOOTBALL X Corps KNOCKOUT COMPETITION: 52nd KINGS beat 13th KINGS 2 Goals to Nil	
	24/9/19		" " 52nd KINGS beat 37th KINGS 2 Goals to 1	
	26/9/19		LEAVE, which up to present had been at rate of 10 O.Rs per day, suspended owing to Rly strike.	
	27/9/19		AMERICAN ARMY CROSS COUNTRY RUN at COBLENZ: 52nd Kings secured second place.	
	27/9/19	22.40	ALARM sounded on discovery of fire in large timber yard adjoining railway station. Battalion paraded promptly & assisted in putting fire out & saving property.	
	30/9/19		RE-ORGANISATION. Battalion reorganised on basis of 4 Companies of 2 Platoons	
	1/9/19 to 30/9/19		BATTN & COY TRAINING carried out. G.M.C. completed with exception of recruits during the month 9 Officers.	
	30/9/19		BATTN STRENGTH. 31 Officers 838 O.R. Ration Strength 29 Officers 540 Other Ranks. 2 Officers attached to I.A.R were demobilised	

1.10.19.

C.S.C.J. Allan
Lt. Col.
Commdg. 52 "Kings"

LANCASHIRE DIV N

Army Form C. 2118.

WAR DIARY
or
INTELLIGENCE SUMMARY
(Erase heading not required.)

Vol I

War Diary (Commencing 15 3/9)
52 Bn. The King's (Liverpool) Regt.

Jan 1920

Army Form C. 2118.

WAR DIARY
or
INTELLIGENCE SUMMARY

(Erase heading not required.)

Instructions regarding War Diaries and Intelligence Summaries are contained in F. S. Regs., Part II. and the Staff Manual respectively. Title Pages will be prepared in manuscript.

Place	Date	Hour	Summary of Events and Information	Remarks and references to Appendices
WOODBRIDGE SUFFOLK.	16/3/19	10.55	Unit entrains for DOVER. 41 Officers. 762. O.Ranks.	
DOVER.		19.00	" detrains	
DUNKIRK	16/3/19	09.00	Embarked for DUNKIRK.	
		12.00	Disembarked and proceeded to No. 3 Camp.	
	17/3/19	09.00	Entrained for GERMANY.	
OBERCASSEL by BONN	19/3/19	07.00	Detrained 41 Officers. 762. O.Ranks.	
	20/3/19		Takes over Billets, Transport Stores of 1st. DORSET Regt.	
	25/3/19		"A" Coy. 52nd. KINGS assumes command of Control Post on Outpost Line, from "C" Coy. 1st. Dorset Regt.	

O/C/O Albau h/ld
(meg 52nd The King's Regt.

LANCASHIRE DIVN

SIEGBURG 3036
sketch reference

Army Form C. 2118.

WAR DIARY
or
INTELLIGENCE SUMMARY.
(Erase heading not required.)

Instructions regarding War Diaries and Intelligence Summaries are contained in F. S. Regs., Part II. and the Staff Manual respectively. Title pages will be prepared in manuscript.

Place	Date	Hour	Summary of Events and Information	Remarks and references to Appendices
DUNKIRK	16.3.19	1400 hrs	Battalion arrived here from Gt YARMOUTH, NORFOLK, ENGLAND via DOVER.	
SIEGBURG-MÜLLDORF.	19.3.19	1200 hrs	Departed from DUNKIRK by train 1450 hrs 17.3.19 via BAILLUEL, ARMENTIERES, LILLE TOURNAI, GELLINGEN, NAMUR, CHARLEROI, HUY, LIÈGE, VERVIERES, to SIEGBURG-MÜLLDORF. Two Companies B + C billeted at SIEGBURG-MÜLLDORF. Two companies A+D billeted at NIEDER-PLEIS	
GEISTINGEN	22.3.19	1400 hrs	Two companies left SIEGBURG-MÜLLDORF for GEISTINGEN. Bath took over left sub sector of Outpost line from 1/5th Border Regt. B Coy placed on left at WARTH, Company placed on right at ROTT. Extension of line from WARTH to ROTT. Bath Headquarters at GEISTINGEN. Two companies left in reserve at NIEDER-PLEIS. (A+D)	
DAMBROICH	24.3.19	1400 hrs	A+D Companies left NIEDER-PLEIS. A company DAMBROICH. D company to billet at GEISTINGEN	
GEISTINGEN	30.3.19	1200 hrs	Major G. DEVLIN 2nd in Command left the Battalion to take over duties at 94th Infantry Brigade. Capt W.G. SWAIN succeeded him	

Lieut. Colonel,
Commanding, 52nd (Grad.) Bn. Manchester Regt.

Army Form C. 2118.

WAR DIARY
or
INTELLIGENCE SUMMARY.
(Erase heading not required.)

Instructions regarding War Diaries and Intelligence Summaries are contained in F.S. Regs., Part II. and the Staff Manual respectively. Title pages will be prepared in manuscript.

Place	Date	Hour	Summary of Events and Information	Remarks and references to Appendices
OBERCASSEL GERMANY	4/4/19	12.30	Lt.Col. C.E.R.G. ALBAN, DSO arrives to take over temporary command.	
	5/4/19		Lt.Col. C.E.R.G. ALBAN D.S.O takes over command of Battalion from Lt.Col J.C. BURNETT D.S.O.	
	6/4/19	10.00	Lt.Col J.C. BURNETT DSO departs to command 2/4 Bn D of W WEST RIDING REGT.	
	7/4/19		C.O. accompanies G.O.C. 1st Infantry Brigade on reconnaissance of outpost line.	
			Brigade letter received informing us of probable general strike in all unoccupied territory	
	9/4/19	09.30	Company Commanders accompany C.O. & Adjutant on reconnaissance of Battalion sector of outpost sector.	
			Divisional order of battle received.	
	10/4/19		Battalion defence scheme drafted	
		18.00	Double sentries posted on all Battalion sentry posts, where hitherto only single sentries were employed.	
	11/4/19	19.00	Majority of Electric power cut off. Outpost company as RÖMINGHOVEN without light.	
		23.20	Wire (URGENT OPERATION PRIORITY) from 1st King's Brigade reporting that both front line battalions without light, & left Battalion states its pilot lead in distance. Immediate action taken i.e. 1 platoon per Company "stood to" in military piequet.	
	12/4/19	20.00	Brevet Lt.Col (Temp. Brig. Gen) A.H. SPOONER .CMG .DSO arrives to take over command of battalion.	
	13/4/19		Brevet Lt. Col A.H SPOONER CMG. DSO assumes command of the Battalion	
		11.30	Information received that Bolshevic element accepted in principle the proposal put at a recent meeting of unoccupied Germany, to kill on one night all Officers (British & French) in occupied territory. Action taken — all Officers to be armed when out after dark — flying patrols on duty throughout the night. Sergian battalion allowed in neutral zone to deal with civil disturbances	
	15/4/19		Major J.M. Hamilton G.S.O to to the O.C. neutral zone to be allowed through outpost company under cover of white flag.	
	18/4/19		Precaution against Bolshevic threat — all Officers to be armed even when actually playing games.	
	19/4/19		Civil police, bank officials & night watchmen to be allowed to carry revolvers.	
	20/4/19		Officers & O.R. to be allowed to pass contact posts if in possession of pass.	
	21/4/19		Site for rifle range approved by B.F.C. Divisional Sports meeting to consider question of summer sports. Attended by C.O.	

D.D. & L., London, E.C.
(A10266) Wt.W5300/P713 750,000 2/16 Sch. 52 Forms/C2118/16

Army Form C. 2118.

WAR DIARY
or
INTELLIGENCE SUMMARY.

Sheet 17

(Erase heading not required.)

Place	Date	Hour	Summary of Events and Information	Remarks and references to Appendices
	24 4/19		6 Officers & 420 O.R Transferred to this Battalion from 53 K.L.R disbanded.	
	26 4/19		4 30x range finished & firing commenced. Further instructions re Bolshevist threat against Officers. Officers not to walk about singly or singly or not to be billeted singly.	
	28 4/19		Drums attend inspection by G.O.C at HANGELAR aerodrome.	
	29 4/19		C & D Companies tea river trip to COBLENZ.	
	30 4/19		Bombing ground sited & work commenced. Battalion strength 65 officers & 1 attached (U.S.M.C) = 56 officers 1184 O.R. 13 " = 1187 O.R.	

A.H. Spooner Lt. Col.
Comdg 52 K.L.R.

Army Form C. 2118.

WAR DIARY
or
INTELLIGENCE SUMMARY.
(Erase heading not required.)

Instructions regarding War Diaries and Intelligence Summaries are contained in F. S. Regs., Part II. and the Staff Manual respectively. Title pages will be prepared in manuscript.

Place	Date	Hour	Summary of Events and Information	Remarks and references to Appendices
OBERCASSEL GERMANY	1/5/19	0800	Practice defence scheme; code word positions raised at 0800. Last company in position, all transport etc, ready by 0930. All communications in-field well & necessary reports in-dispatched with promptitude.	
	2/5/19	14:30	Conference with G.O.C. Div. at Rlys Brigade H.Q. of defence scheme. C.O., 2I/C, Adjutant, & O.C. Companies attended.	
	4/5/19		Weather:- Rise in temperature - ground drying quickly	
	7/5/19		Major C.E.R.L. Allan D.S.C. assumes command of the Battalion this day vice Lt Col M.A.S.Roche D.M.G. D.S.C. proceeded to take over command of 13th R.F.	
	8/5/19		Outpost line advanced to include DOLLENDORFER HARDT.	
	13/5/19		Battalion Armourer present at C-in-C's inspection of units of Rhine Riv. at HAMAKIAR MEDO DROME.	
	14/5/19		"B" Company mount Divisional Guard at BONN.	
	16/5/19		Marshal Foch visits British forces by river from COBLENZ. Battalion paraded in full length on the right bank.	
	18/5/19		Officers moun lid hopper chiset, 24 skaters.	
	23/5/19		Brigadier inspects "A" Company in tactical scheme.	
	27/5/19		Test route march of 10 miles, F.M.O.	
	1-5-19 to 31-5-19		Individual & Platoon training carried out. Battalion Strength - Officers 4.9. & 2 attached. O.R. 1163. + 3 attached.	

C E R G Allan
Lieut Colonel
Cmdg. 12nd Bn. The Rifles.

(A10260) Wt. W5300/P713 750,000 2/18 **Sch. 52** Forms/C2118/16

Army Form C. 2118.

WAR DIARY
or
INTELLIGENCE SUMMARY.
(Erase heading not required.)

Place	Date	Hour	Summary of Events and Information	Remarks and references to Appendices
OBERCASSEL GERMANY	3/6/19		Special battalion parade in honour of the King's Birthday. Inter-company musketry competitions on 200x range.	
"	12/6/19. 13/6/19		Brigade Rifle Meeting on 200x range. 52 King's won 2 Battalion competitions	
"	14/6/19 15/6/19		Musketry & sports meeting 52 King's v 51 Manchesters at BIRLINGHOVEN. 52 King's won by 1 point.	
"	17/6/19		Confirmation of J day received. Action taken in accordance with orders previously issued.	
"	18/6/19		All surplus stores kits etc taken to rear dumps at BONN. (J-2 day)	
BIRLINGHOVEN	19/6/19		"J"- 1 day. Battalion moves to BIRLINGHOVEN - less D Coy, who remain on outpost duty at RÖMLINGHOVEN. Leave OBERCASSEL 10·10 hours, fighting order arrive BIRLINGHOVEN 12·00 hours. Troops in close billets for the night.	
"	29/6/19.	19·00	Peace treaty signed. News received 18·00 hours.	
"	19/19 - 29/6/19		Company & specialist training carried out at BIRLINGHOVEN	
OBERCASSEL	30/6/19.		"A" day. Battalion returns to original billets in OBERCASSEL.	
			STRENGTH OF BATTALION ON 30/6/19 - OFFICERS 48 - 2 ATTACHED O.R. 1123 - 2 "	

(Signed) A.Brown Lt.Col.
Comdg 52nd The King's Regt.

Army Form C. 2118.

WAR DIARY
or
INTELLIGENCE SUMMARY.
(Erase heading not required.)

July 1919

Instructions regarding War Diaries and Intelligence Summaries are contained in F. S. Regs., Part II. and the Staff Manual respectively. Title pages will be prepared in manuscript.

Place	Date	Hour	Summary of Events and Information	Remarks and references to Appendices
OBERCASSEL GERMANY	2-4/7/19		Brigade Rifle Meeting on RAMERSDORF range — no inter-battalion events. 52nd King's obtained 4 firsts, 1 second & 1 third place; and a large majority of individual competitions.	
	5/7/19		"B" Company sports.	
	6/7/19		"C" Company sports.	
	7/7/19		The Commanding Officer proceeds to Paris as A.D.C. to J.J. Commanding Rhine Army troops taking part in the PARIS VICTORY MARCH. Major J.H. Lotham assumes command of the battalion.	
	9/7/19		Four W.O.'s & N.C.O.'s proceeded to Paris to represent this battalion in the Victory march. Brigade Boxing Competition, won by 52nd King's.	
	15/7/19		Brigade swimming competition & water polo match won by 52nd King's.	
	17/7/19		A & B companies proceed on Rhine trip.	
	18/7/19		Lt. Col. Allan DSO returns from Paris & assumes command of the battalion.	
	21/7/19		Successful battalion sports held at RÖMLINGHOVEN. Inter-company sports cup was won by D company.	
	23/7/19		Brigade Sports meeting. The battalion obtained first place in the following events:— Mile relay race, Cross country race, Tug of war & Transport. The battalion was presented with the Brigade Commander's shield which was won by a margin of six points.	
	25/7/19		Major J.H. Lotham assumes command of the battalion vice Lt. Col. Allan DSO proceeded on leave to U.K.	
	1-31/7/19		Battalion & company training out. G.M.C. commenced on RAMERSDORF RANGE.	
	31/7/19		Battalion strength. OFFICERS 48 & 2 attached O.R. 1073.	

R. Allen
Lieut for Major
Cmdg. 52nd Bn "The King's" Liverpool Regt.

Army Form C. 2118.

WAR DIARY
or
INTELLIGENCE SUMMARY.
(Erase heading not required.)

Instructions regarding War Diaries and Intelligence Summaries are contained in F. S. Regs., Part II. and the Staff Manual respectively. Title pages will be prepared in manuscript.

Place	Date	Hour	Summary of Events and Information	Remarks and references to Appendices
OBERCASSEL-GERMANY.	5.8.19.		Brigade Hockey Match : 13th Kings beat 52nd Kings. 1-0.	
	10.8.19.		Divisional Challenge Cup : Tug of War : Heavy weight. 52nd Kings beat 13th Kings. Light weight. 52nd Kings beat 13th Kings.	
	14.8.19.		Battalion proceeded on Rhine trip to COBLENZ	
	16.8.19.		"A" Company took over Outpost line duties at VINXEL.	
	18.8.19.		Lt. Col. C. J. R. G. Alban, DSO. resumed command of Battalion on return from leave.	
			1 officer & 5 other ranks proceeded on tour of ARRAS Battlefields.	
	22.8.19.		Divisional Cross Country Run : 52nd. Kings gained 2nd. place.	
	27.8.19.		Divisional Horse Show : 52nd. Kings gained 1 first (Officers Ride & Drive) & 2 thirds.	
	31.8.19.		Presentation of medals by G.O.C. Brigade to winners in Brigade Sports.	
	1-31.8.19.		Battalion & Company training carried out.	
			"A" & "C" Companies completed G.M.C.	
			"B" Company commenced G.M.C.	
	31.8.19.		Battalion Strength : 47 Officers. 1006 Other Ranks.	
			2 Officers attached.	

C/Col. Alban h C2
Comdg 52 The King's Regt

Army Form C. 2118.

WAR DIARY
or
INTELLIGENCE SUMMARY.
(Erase heading not required.)

Instructions regarding War Diaries and Intelligence Summaries are contained in F.S. Regs., Part II. and the Staff Manual respectively. Title pages will be prepared in manuscript.

Place	Date	Hour	Summary of Events and Information	Remarks and references to Appendices
OBERCASSEL.	8/9 to 13/9/19		RHINE ARMY RIFLE MEETING. 52nd Kings succeeded in winning 4 Cups (3 firsts 1 second) + 45 Medals.	
	16/9.19.		TUG OF WAR. 52nd Kings beat 5th Borderers thus winning Divisional Final.	
	17/9.19.		TUG OF WAR. 63rd R.G.A. beat 52nd Kings in Army Semi-Final.	
	22/9.19.		CORPS AQUATIC SPORTS: 52nd Kings won: - 2 Firsts: 2 Seconds + 1 Third.	
	23/9.19.		FOOTBALL Xth CORPS KNOCKOUT COMPETITION 52nd Kings beat 13th Kings 2 Goals to Nil	
	24/9.19		" " 52nd Kings beat 51st Kings 2 Goals to 1.	
	26/9.19.		LEAVE, which up to present had been at rate of 10 per day suspended owing to strike.	
	27/9.19.		AMERICAN ARMY CROSS COUNTRY RUN at Coblenz. 52nd Kings secured second place.	
	27/9.19. 22.40		ALARM sounded on discovery of fire in large timber yard adjoining Railway Station. Battn. posted picquets + assisted in putting fire out + saving property.	
	30/9.19.		RE-ORGANISATION. Battalion re-organised on basis of 4 Companies of 2 Platoons.	
	1/9.19. to 30/9.19.		BATTN. COY TRAINING carried out.	
	30/9.19.		G.M.C. Completed with exception of casuals.	
			During the month 9 Officers + 157 O.R. were demobilised.	
	30/9.19.		BATTN. STRENGTH 37 Officers + 839 O.R. Ration Strength {Officers 29, Other Ranks 540} 2 Officers attacked.	1.10.19

(VRGRUrau)
Lieut Col.
Commdg. 52 Kings.

Army Form C. 2118.

WAR DIARY
or
INTELLIGENCE SUMMARY

(Erase heading not required.)

October 1919.

Instructions regarding War Diaries and Intelligence Summaries are contained in F. S. Regs., Part II. and the Staff Manual respectively. Title Pages will be prepared in manuscript.

Place	Date October	Hour	Summary of Events and Information	Remarks and references to Appendices
OBERCASSEL	4		X Corps Association Knock-out Competition, 3rd Round 52nd King's 4 Goals – 32nd M.G.C. 2 goals.	
	7		Bn. Rugby football team beaten by 13th K.L.R. (8-3) in first match of season.	
	11		X Corps Association knock-out semi-final, 5th Borders 3 – 52nd King's 1.	
	13		Hockey :- 12th L.N.L. 5 Goals – 52nd King's 4.	
	14		X Corps Rugger knock-out, 52nd King's 8 – 15th L.F.'s 6 points.	
	17		52nd King's move from Obercassel to Infantry Barracks, Bonn – Move orders attached –	
	18		Battalion takes over town duties & picquets & mounts Corps Commanders Guard of 6 N.C.O.s & 18 O.R.	
	20		Lieut Col A.H. Spooner C.M.G. D.S.O. takes command of the battalion, & Lt Col. C.E.R.J. Allan D.S.O. retains command while Lt Col Spooner is in command of 2nd Lancs. Inf: Brigade.	
	20		G.H.Q. wire urgent for Commanding Officer. Informed that the battalion was to prepare to move to FLENSBORG – SCHLESWIG-HOLSTEIN; preparations to be complete by 30th Inst. Preparations for a 3 months detachment to be made, & 3 months supplies to be taken.	
	21		Re-inforcements of 132 O.R.'s (men under 21 years) arrived from 13th K.L.R.	
	23		Re-inforcements of 229 O.R.'s (men under 21 years) arrived from 51st K.L.R.	
	24		Officer re-inforcements to complete establishment 6 from 13th K.L.R. & 2 from 51st K.L.R.	
	24		X Corps rugby football semi-final :- X Corps Troops beat 52nd K.L.R.	
	27		Action in case of riots in BONN. Practice Alarm – orders attached –	
	28		Hockey :- 52nd King's 3 – 12th L.N.L. 0.	
	31		Orders to move to FLENSBORG on 3/11/19 received. Capt W.E. Foss M.C. proceeded to FLENSBORG to prepare for arrival of Battalion. Companies re-organised on a 4 Platoon basis. Section & platoon training carried out.	
	31		4 Officers & 34 O.R.'s demobilized during the month. Battalion Total Strength Officers 40-1 attached. O.R.'s 1191-1 attached. Battalion Ration Strength 35-1 " – " : 1042-1 " – "	

C.R.J. Allan
Lieut. Col.
Comdg 52nd Bn. "The King's" (L'pool Regt).

SECRET.   COPY NO. 20
              52nd. Bn. "THE KING'S".
                Order No. 4.

1. The 52nd. King's will move to the BONNER TALWEG BARRACKS, BONN on
   Friday the 17th. inst. The Battalion will take over the billets
   at present occupied by the 12th. Bn. Loyal North Lancs. The 51st.
   K.L.R. will take over billets and Outposts from this Battalion.

2. The Battalion will parade in full marching order (Drums in
   fighting order) in the following order - H.Q., B, Drums, C, D,
   Transport. Head of column will pass the starting point, Grammar
   School, OBERCASSEL, at 10.30 hours. Company Cookers and Lewis
   Gun Limbers (except "A" Company) will march with Transport.
   "A" Company will proceed independantly after relief.

3. a. One Officer per Company and H.Q. will remain behind to hand over
      billets, Outposts, etc., to incoming Units. This Officer must
      get the following signed by Officer taking over -

         1. Clean billet certificate (in triplicate).
         2. List of existing damages (in triplicate).
         3. Outpost Companies - receipt for all stores, etc., handed over.
         4. List of requisitioned stores handed over.

   b. Outpost Companies will remain until relieved by incoming Unit.

4. a. Advance parties composed as under will proceed by the 0820
      electric train -

      1. Per Company.   1 C.Q.M.S.
                         Company Cooks with rations to prepare dinners.
                         1 N.C.O. per platoon.

      2. Orderly Room.   Asst. Adjt., 1 N.C.O. and 1 Clerk.

      3. Q.M. will detail his own advance party

      4. Sergeants' Mess Caterer.

      5. Messing Officer.

   b. Officers' Mess. There will be a Battalion Officers' Mess at the
      new station. Officers' Mess waiters of all Companies will report
      to Sgt. Wood at ROMLINGHOVEN Station at 0910 hours.

5. Q.M. will take over on Morning of the 17th. from 12th. L.N.L. a
   list of existing barrack damages, and will sign cleanliness
   certificate if all is in order.

6. a. Lorries will report as under -

                          Place.   Time.
      "A" Company.   Company Office.   08.00 hours.
      "B"   "   do.   do.   do.   do.
      "C"   "   do   do   do   do
      "D"   "   do   do   do   do
      H.Q.   Orderly Room.   do   do to include
                                                 Education Stores.
      Q.M.   Q.M. Stores.   do   do

52nd. Bn. "THE KING'S" Order No. 4, Sheet 2.
---

6. (Cntd.).

1 man of "A" and 1 of "D" Coys. will report to Q.M. Stores at 07.45 hours to guide lorries to respective Companies.

b. Companies will be responsible for loading kits, blankets, stores, etc., at this end and a fatigue party will accompany the lorry to off-load and guard kits at BONN.

c. O.C. "B" Company will detail a fatigue party of 1 N.C.O. and 12 men to load and off-load Q.M. Stores' lorry.

d. Officers' kits will be taken on respective Company lorries. H.Q. Officers' kits will be dumped at 0800 hours at B.O.R. or H.Q. Coy. office.

e. Transport will carry Bn. L.G. and Signalling stores and kits, blankets, etc., of Transport Section.

7. B.O.R. will close at OBERCASSEL at 10.30 hours and open at that hours at the new quarters.

8. Station Control - Orders for Station Control will be issued later.

9. ACKNOWLEDGE.

NOTE. It may be necessary to alter the time of the move on receipt of further instructions. Any alteration will be communicated to all concerned in an addendum to this order.

R. Hick
Lieut., & A/Adjt.,
52nd. Bn. "The King's".

OBERCASSEL.
15.10.1919.

Copy No.
1 to Brigade.
2 to "A" Company.
3 to "B" "
4 to "C" "
5 to "D" "
6 to H.Q.
7 to Transport Officer.
8 to Quartermaster.
9 to Education Officer.
10 to Station Control Post.
11 to Major Latham.
12 to Asst. Adjutant.
13 to R.S.M.
14 to Messing Officer.
15 to 12th. Bn. L.N.L.
16 to 51st. Bn. W.L.R.
17 to Medical Officer.
18 to Lewis Gun Officer.
19 File.
20. War Diary

SECRET. 52ND KING'S. COPY NO.....

ADDENDUM NO. 1 TO ORDER NO. 4.

ORDER No. 4:—
The following alterations are to be made in HOME

Para. 3 add:—

(c) "B" Coy. 51st. K.L.R. will arrive at ROLLINGHOVEN about 09.30 hours. "D" Coy. will march out after relief, in sufficient time to pass starting point at 10.30 hours.

Para. 4 (a) 1. Re company Cooks, substitute:—
"B", "C", "D" & "H.Q" Coy. Cooks will report to Q. stores at 08.00 hours prompt.

Para. 6 (c) The following additional fatigue parties are required. They will proceed by the 08.20 train in full marching order, and will not return to OBERCASSEL.
"B" 1 N.C.O. & 12 men.
"C" 1 N.C.O. & 12 men.
"D" 1 N.C.O. & 6 men.
On arrival at the BONNER TALWEG BARRACKS the senior N.C.O. will report arrival to Q.M. 18th. L.N.L.R. The parties are required for loading fatigues.

Para. 8 Substitute :— The Station Control Post personnel will remain in present position pending further instructions.
After Friday 17th. inst. they will be rationed by 51st. K.L.R.

ACKNOWLEDGE.

R. Thir

Lieut. & A/Adjt.,
52nd. Bn. "The King's".

OBERCASSEL.
14-10-19.

Copy No. 1 to Brigade.   11 to Major Latham.
         2 to "A" Company.   12 to Asst. Adjutant.
         3 to "B"   "   13 to R.S.M.
         4 to "C"   "   14 to Messing Officer.
         5 to "D"   "   15 to 18th.Bn.L.N.L.
         6 to H.Q.   "   16 to 51st.Bn.K.L.R.
         7 to Transport Officer. 17 to Medical Officer.
         8 to Quartermaster.   18 to Lewis Gun Officer.
         9 to Education Officer. 19 File.
        10 to Station Control Post 20 WAR DIARY

52nd. Bn. "The Kings" Liverpool Regt.

S E C R E T.   Order No. 1.   Copy. No. 9.

1. There will in all probability be a trial alarm tomorrow to practice the defence of BONN in case of riots.

2. On receipt of the code word "RIOTS" the following will take effect

3. The battalion will parade in mass on the square in Fighting Order - 60 rounds S.A.A. per man will be carried and the remaining 60 rounds per man will be stacked in bulk by companies on the square.

4. (a) "D" Company will find the Town Picket which will be doubled- i.e. full company. They will proceed to the A? HOF and come under order of the A.P.M.
    (b) Half "A" Company will proceed to the Bonn Goods Station to guard stores etc.
    (c) 2 platoons of "B" Company will proceed to the Bonn Bridge and will be located in the guard room (last house on right before crossing bridge). They will find a guard at each end of the Bridge - strength to be decided by senior officer.

5. No Lewis Guns will be taken but all officers and other ranks will know where the guns would be placed if being used.

6. The Quarter-Guard on the barracks will be doubled and the police will remain in barracks. The Company staffs, Orderly Room Staff and Q.? Staff will be responsible for the guarding of their own stores.

7. The drums will parade with their own companies in Fighting Order.

8. The Transport will be ready to move stores, rations etc. if requi

9. The report centre will be the RATHAUS and Companies will report when in position.

10. Acknowledge.

H.Marshall

Capt. & Adjutant.
52nd. Bn. "The Kings"

26.10.1919.

Copy. No. 1. to O.C. "A" Company.
       2.   "B"   "
       3.   "C"   "
       4.   "D"   "
       5.   "H.Q" "
       6.   C.O.
       7.   Major F.W. Latham.
       8.   Adjutant.
       9.   War Diary.
      10.   War Diary.
      11.   Transport Officer.
      12.   Q.M.
      13.   R.S.M.
      14.   Lewis Gun Officer.

52nd Bn King's Liverpool Regt.

SECRET.

Order No 2   Copy No. 9.

Further to this Office Order No 1 of to-day's date.

1. The alarm will sound at 0830 hours, unless further instructions are received.

2. The instructions contained in above order will be carried out on sound of the alarm.

3. The extra 60 rounds per man will be issued out before 0830 hours to-morrow and each man will carry 120 rnds on parade.

4. Acknowledge.

26/10/19.

H.Marshall
Capt & Adjutant.
52nd Bn King's L'pool Regt.

Copy No 1 to O.C. "A" Company.
    2   "B"
    3   "C"
    4   "D"
    5   H.Q.
    6   C.O.
    7   Major F.W.Latham.
    8   Adjutant.
    9   War Diary.
   10   War Diary.
   11   Transport Officer.
   12   Q.M.
   13   R.S.M.
   14   L.Gun Officer.

52nd Bn King's Liverpool Regiment.

S E C R E T.   ORDER NO. 3   Copy.No. 9

Ref Order No 1 issued to-day. This is cancelled and the following substituted.

1. The "Alarm" will not be sounded but the Battalion will parade in Fighting Order, (Steel Helmets and Box Respirators in the alert position), on the square at 0930 hours, Officers to wear the same order as the men.

2. The half Company of "A" Company will proceed as instructed, parading on Square at 0845 hours.

3. The Town picquet to be found by "D" Company will not proceed to the AM HOF but will parade on the Square at 0930 hours. Two seperate detachments of 3 Officers and 80 O.Ranks each being formed, one to represent the Town picquet on duty and the other the doubling of this.
The remainder of the Company will be attached to "C" Company.

4. The 2 platoons of "B" Company will march to BONN BRIDGE as directed. All troops of 13th K.L.R. will be used as the Company for the immediate defence of the bridge.
The Officer in command of the 2 platoons of "B" Company will be in charge of the whole.

5. The H.Q. will not move to the RATHAUS but will remain in the Barracks.

6. British ladies will not concentrate at the KONIGSHOF.

7. Only 60 rounds per man will be carried and not 120 rounds.

8. The Corps Commander will inspect the arrangements at the following times - After inspection detachments will march back to the Barracks.

Infantry Barracks	-	1010 hours.
Bonn Bridge	-	1110 hours
Goods Station	-	1150 hours.

9. Acknowledge.

26.10.19.

HVM

Capt. & Adjt.
52nd Bn King's.

Copy No 1 to O.C."A" Company.
        2   "B"
        3   "C"
        4   "D"
        5   H.Q.
        6   C.O.
        7   Major F.W.Latham.

Copy 8 to Adjutant.
     9   War Diary.
    10   War Diary.
    11   Transport Officer.
    12   Q.M.
    13   R.S.M.
    14   L.G.Officer.

www.ingramcontent.com/pod-product-compliance
Lightning Source LLC
Chambersburg PA
CBHW081250170426
43191CB00037B/2102